THE HARLEQUIN MOTH

ITS LIFE STORY BY MILLICENT E. SELSAM

WITH PHOTOGRAPHS BY JEROME WEXLER

William Morrow and Company   New York 1975

The author and photographer thank
John C. Pallister,
Research Assistant in the Department of Entomology,
American Museum of Natural History,
for checking the text and photographs of this book.

ACKNOWLEDGMENTS FOR PHOTOGRAPHS
Lynwood M. Chace, National Audubon Society, 45, 47
Leonard Lee Rue III, National Audubon Society, 44
Hugh Spencer, National Audubon Society, 41, 42

Text copyright © 1975 by Millicent E. Selsam
Photographs copyright © 1975 by Jerome Wexler

Printed in the United States of America.

1 2 3 4 5 79 78 77 76 75

Library of Congress Cataloging in Publication Data

Selsam, Millicent Ellis (date)
   The harlequin moth.

   1. Euchaetius egle—Juvenile literature.
I. Wexler, Jerome. II. Title.
QL561.A8S44   595.7′81   75-17862
ISBN 0-688-22049-5
ISBN 0-688-32049-X lib. bdg.

This is the life story of an ordinary moth.
It lives on the milkweed plant.
Its common name is harlequin moth;
its scientific name is *Euchaetias egle.*
The moth is only the last stage
in a long series of changes that starts with the egg.

A good place to look for the eggs
of the harlequin moth is on a milkweed plant.

Here is a milkweed leaf
with a circle of cotton on it.

Under the cotton are the eggs of the moth.

Here is a close-up view of the eggs.
You can see the yellowish-white yolk of the eggs
and the caterpillars growing inside the eggs.
The egg in the center
is not developing like the others.

In this picture
a single egg is held
at the tip of a pin.
You can see the head
of the caterpillar inside.

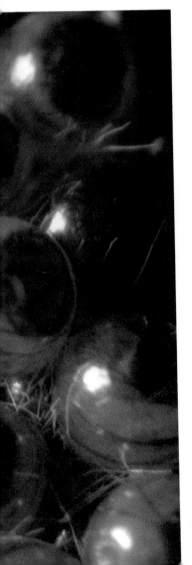

Now the eggs have hatched
into tiny caterpillars.
They are crawling all over the leaf.
Notice their black heads.

The caterpillars have strong jaws
with which they crunch the leaves.

The caterpillars leave their droppings
on the leaves below them.
You can find the caterpillars
if you look on the underside of the leaf
above the leaf with the droppings.

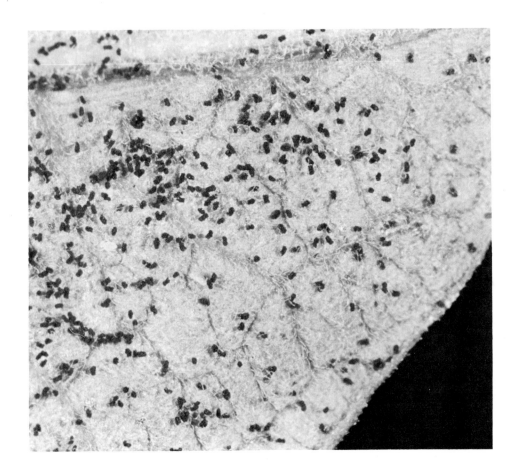

Three days later
the caterpillars have doubled in size.
Now they stop eating
and gather together.
They rest for a day or two.

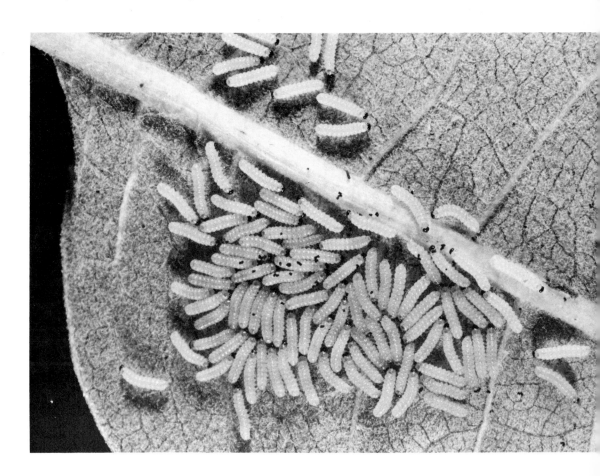

Caterpillars eat so much and get so fat
that they burst their old skins.
In the case of the caterpillars
of the harlequin moth,
they shed their skins five times.
Each time the caterpillar
wriggles out of the old split skin,
and each time
it has a new, bigger skin underneath.
The process is called "molting."

In the picture to the right,
you see the first molt.

1 caterpillar about to molt
2 caterpillar in act of molting
3 caterpillar just after molting
4 cast-off skin

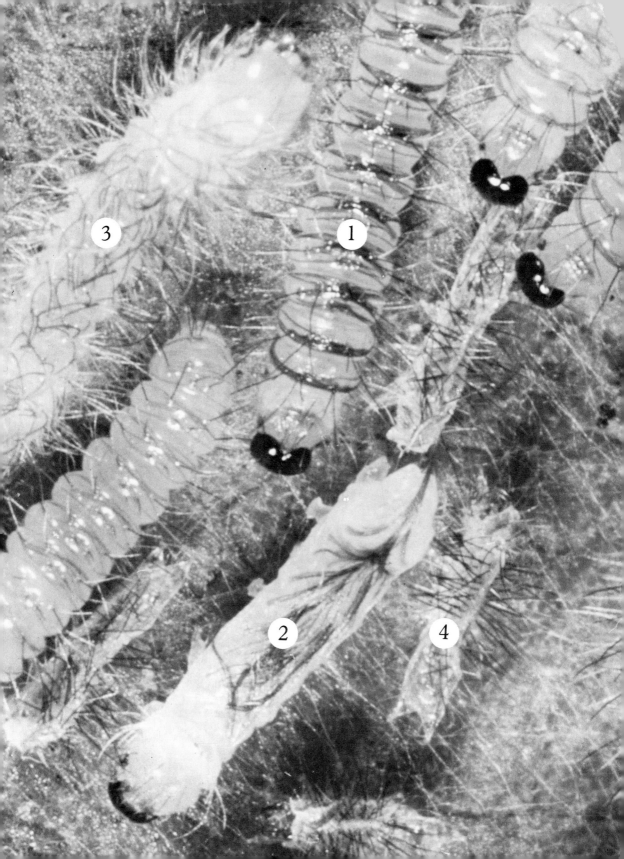

After a while the caterpillar shows
rings of black dots and the head darkens.

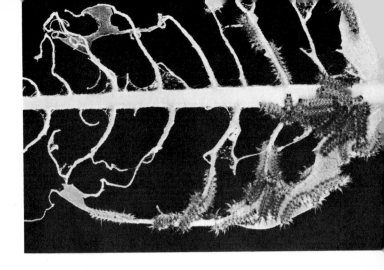

The caterpillars
go back to eating
the leaves again.

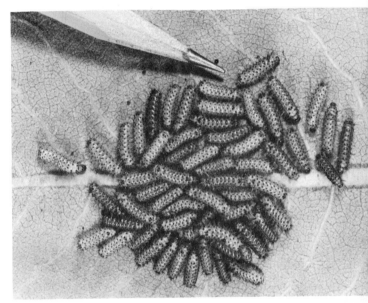

After two days
of eating,
the caterpillars
gather together.
They rest before
the second molt.

When they shed
their skins this time,
the caterpillars
are all black
and quite hairy.

15

The black hairy
caterpillars
continue to eat
the leaves
of the milkweed.
Then they gather
together again
to rest before
the next molt.
This one is
the third molt.

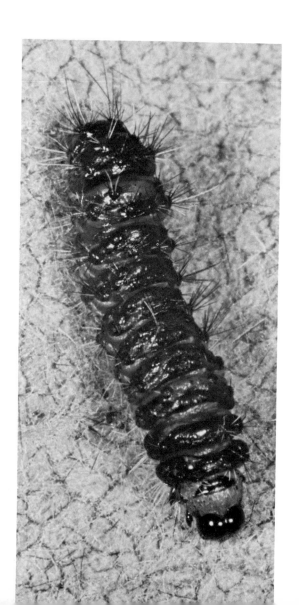

The caterpillar
is pulling out
of its black skin.

The light part
in front
is its head.
The old head mask
is falling off. ►

Now it is out.
To dry itself off,
it twists over and over.
It looks like
a ball of hair.
Notice the head mask
lying beside it.

The caterpillar's hairs
have dried out.
It is not black anymore.
It now has the bright
harlequin colors
that give this caterpillar
its name.

The caterpillars
keep eating
and eating.
They gather
together again
to rest before
the fourth molt.

The caterpillar
has just completed
its fourth molt.
The old head mask
and the old skin
are lying beside it.
It has the same
harlequin colors
as before.

Once more the caterpillars eat leaves.
For six days they devour the milkweed leaves.

Finally they stop for the fifth and last molt.
In the following series of pictures
showing the fifth molt,
you can see exactly how the caterpillar
wriggles out of its old skin.

The legs of the old skin dig into a leaf or branch
and remain fixed as the caterpillar crawls out.
First it pushes up against the front of the old skin.
The old skin stretches and separates behind the head.

When the head mask
falls off,
you can see
the new head.

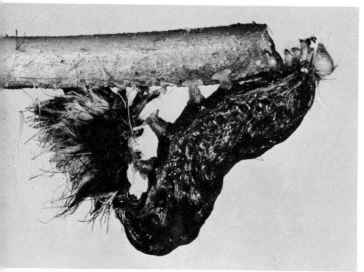

The caterpillar
keeps pushing its way
out of the old skin.

The old skin
is left behind.

The caterpillar
rolls and twists
to dry off its hair.

The caterpillar crawls away.
It still has the harlequin colors,
but it is bigger.
In a day or two the head turns black.

Here you can get an idea of its real size.

The caterpillars are full grown now.
They tickle as they crawl up a bare arm.

Again the caterpillars stop eating and rest.
But this time they scatter and look for quiet spots.
When they find the right place,
they start to pull hair out of their backs.
At the same time, silk comes out of their mouths
from a little tube on the lower lip.
It is called a "spinneret"
and is connected with glands that make the silk
inside the caterpillar's body.
With these materials the caterpillar forms
a protective covering for itself called a "cocoon."

In this picture
and the ones on the next page,
the cocoon was made
in a paper box.
But out of doors the caterpillars
crawl off the milkweed plant
and find a place on the ground.
They use whatever they find
on the ground—whether sand
or bits of leaves and twigs—
and make it part of their cocoon.

The caterpillar
continues to weave
the silk and hairs
together
until the cocoon
is finished.

But what is happening inside the cocoon?
This caterpillar was taken out of the cocoon
so you can see.
The caterpillar lies very still at first.

Then it begins to twitch,
and the body stretches in wavelike motions
toward the head.
The light bands show where the skin is stretching.

Then suddenly there is a split behind the head.

The split gets
bigger and bigger.

The caterpillar skin
is almost off.

The old skin
is left behind.

31

Now you see something new.
It is called a "pupa."
At first it is cream white and very soft.

Then it darkens and hardens.
You can see wings forming.

All these changes take place
inside the hairy cocoon.

The cocoon lies on the ground all winter.
But within a new series of changes takes place.
The pupa turns into a full-grown adult moth.
Here the moth's head
is pushing its way out of the cocoon.

In this picture the pupa case
was taken out of the cocoon
so that you can see how it breaks open
to release the moth.
At first the moth has small crumpled wings.

But soon the moth
climbs up a stick
or branch—
whatever is near—
and pumps up
its wings
with blood.
Slowly
the moth's wings
get bigger
and bigger.

In the picture
to the right
the wings are
almost full size.

At last the full-grown moth appears!

What a long series of changes must take place
before it becomes an adult moth.
These changes from the egg to the caterpillar
to the pupa to the adult moth
are called "metamorphosis."

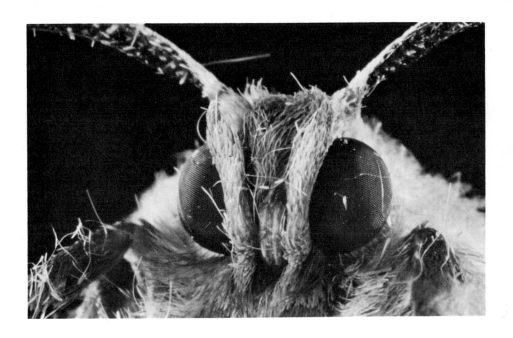

Here is a close-up of the female moth's head.
Notice the two huge eyes.
Two antennae stick out of the top of its head.
On the antennae are organs of feeling and smelling.

The antennae of male moths are usually feathery
and have very sensitive smell organs.
With them, a moth can smell a female from far away.
The female gives off a scent
from glands in her abdomen.
The wind carries the tiny scent particles
from the female moth.

head of a male
gypsy moth

The male moth heads straight into the wind
that carries the scent.
He follows it as it gets stronger and stronger.
Finally he reaches her.

Then male and female moths mate.
In the process of mating,
the male moth
presses sperm
into her abdomen
where the eggs are.
When the sperm
join the eggs,
the eggs are fertilized
and can start to develop.
The egg on page 6,
which did not develop
like the others,
was not fertilized.
Only when the eggs
are fertilized
can they change
into caterpillars
that change
into pupae
that change
into adult moths
that mate and lay eggs
and start the cycle
again.

cecropia moths mating

The caterpillars of the harlequin moth
usually feed on milkweed plants
that are not useful to man.
Among the other caterpillars,
at least one is helpful,
but some can do a lot of harm.

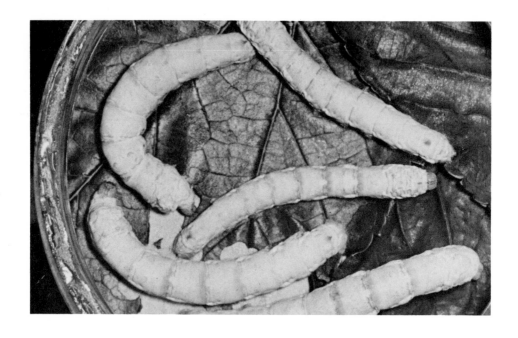

SILKWORM MOTH
The caterpillar of this moth is very useful.
It spins a silky cocoon,
from which silk thread and cloth are made.

TENT CATERPILLAR

One nest of these caterpillars can eat
all the leaves of a small tree.
The caterpillars get their names
from the silk tent that they weave
in a fork of a tree.
They live together in the tent
and go forth to feed when it is not too hot.

GYPSY MOTH

This caterpillar eats the leaves
of fruit and shade trees.
It came here from Europe
in connection with some experiments done in 1869.
Some of the specimens escaped
and have now spread all over
the New England states.
See if you can find the caterpillars
eating the leaves.

44

TOMATO HORNWORM

Anyone who has grown tomatoes
has seen this fat green caterpillar
with white diagonal stripes along its sides
and a sort of "tail" at the end.
If you notice big holes in the leaves
of the tomato plant, look carefully
for tomato hornworms and pick them off.
Otherwise, they will strip
the whole plant of its leaves.

CORN EARWORM

Many times you may see this caterpillar
when you pull down the husk to check
if you have selected a good ear of corn.
The corn earworm not only attacks corn,
it feeds on tomato, beans, and other crops.

46

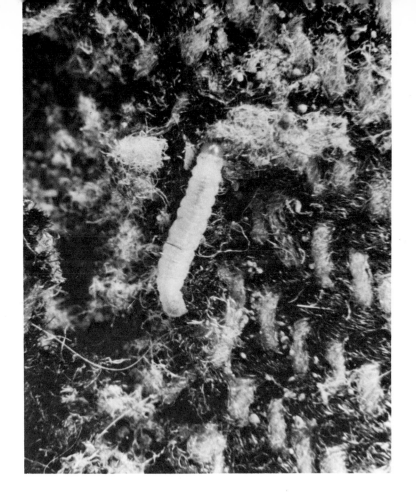

CLOTHES MOTH

The caterpillars of this moth make holes
in our woolens, furs, and sometimes silk.
The clothes moths you sometimes see
flying around are not harmful,
for they eat nothing in the adult state.
But the females do lay eggs
that change into caterpillars.

47

Whether a moth is helpful or harmful,
learning its life history is important.
If you know where and when its eggs are laid,
what the caterpillars feed on,
and where and how they spend the winter,
you are better able to control or use them.